PUF

Staying Co
How to Su

Rosie Rushton lives in Northampt—
knows only too well how unprepared many chil...
when going to secondary school. She was a feature writer for
her local newspaper before turning freelance and has
contributed to most of the women's national magazines. This
is her first book.

Kathryn Lamb lives in Dorset with her husband, Adrian
Dovey, and has four children and three stepchildren. After
studying English at Oxford, her hobby, drawing, turned into
her career. She has illustrated numerous children's books,
often working in collaboration with Adrian.

Staying Cool,
Surviving School

How to Survive Secondary School

ROSIE RUSHTON

Illustrated by
Kathryn Lamb

PUFFIN BOOKS

PUFFIN BOOKS

Published by the Penguin Group
Penguin Books Ltd, 27 Wrights Lane, London W8 5TZ, England
Penguin Books USA Inc., 375 Hudson Street, New York, New York 10014, USA
Penguin Books Australia Ltd, Ringwood, Victoria, Australia
Penguin Books Canada Ltd, 10 Alcorn Avenue, Toronto, Ontario, Canada M4V 3B2
Penguin Books (NZ) Ltd, 182–190 Wairau Road, Auckland 10, New Zealand

Penguin Books Ltd, Registered Offices: Harmondsworth, Middlesex, England

First published by Piccadilly Press Ltd 1993
Published in Puffin Books 1995
1 3 5 7 9 10 8 6 4 2

CONTENTS

WARNING!
All would-be Secondary school survivors take note!

WITHOUT wishing to upset the even tempo of your life, you should know that halfway through your last year in junior school, most of the familiar figures in your life will undergo some rather worrying changes. Your parents will suddenly start fixing expressions of doom on their ageing faces and begin to say things like, "When you get to the Comprehensive, you won't be able to sit around all evening watching television, you know," and "It's high time you realised that there is a real world out there!" (What do they think you imagine you have been living in for the last decade or so – Legoland?)

Teachers begin to give you pep talks around 3 pm every afternoon – something along the lines of, "Here at Homeforth First/Middle School we have been one big happy family. Now the time is coming when you must leave these familiar walls to go on to pastures new, to take on bigger challenges and greater responsibilities. And, of course, to work hard so that in a few years' time you are equipped to fight for a place in the ever-shrinking job market."

The same parents and teachers who utter such jolly predictions then wonder why you are not leaping up and down in excitement at the thought of going to secondary school. Ten minutes after telling you that you will have hours of homework, two cross-country runs every week and a BCG vaccination, they remark, "What are you worrying about? You'll love it." Which just goes to show how inconsistent adults can be.

All is not doom and gloom, however. With a little bit of advance planning and a great deal of careful observation in your first year, you can get the system sussed and have it working to your advantage. Which is where this book comes in. Keep it between your Concise Dictionary of French Language and the copy of Practical Biology and you won't go far wrong. Just make sure the teachers don't get hold of it. Apart from not wanting them to understand your strategies, they hate to discover that their pupils have got the measure of them. It rather deflates their egos and you can bet your life, you will be the one to suffer for it.

So pack your kit bag, grab the solar-powered calculator and Save The Tiger ring binder and head for the school bus. You never know – you might actually enjoy it.

Chapter One
CHOOSING A SCHOOL

"School is where you go between when your parents can't take you and industry can't take you."
(John Updike)

In the old days, kids didn't get a lot of choice about where they went to school. Each area had its primary school and that fed one secondary school, along with a grammar school for the brainboxes, and that was where you went. But all that is changing.

WHAT'S ON OFFER?

1. In the majority of schools, the governors and the Head run the place, but the local authority tells them how much they can spend and when. In most areas, the majority of state schools are co-educational, but most places have a single-sex one as well - it's up to you and your parents to decide which is best for you.

2. Then there are grant–maintained schools, which are run completely independently of the local council and get their cash from the government. This is what opting out means – sorry, it doesn't mean they have thrown in the towel and decided on no more Maths tests.

3. In cities there is a new type of school called City Technology Colleges, or CTCs. These have special emphasis on science and technology and often have help from local businesses.

4. Then there are independent schools. You don't have to be rolling in cash and living in a country mansion to go because if you are clever you may well qualify for an Assisted Place and your parents get help with the fees – or sometimes get them waived altogether. So don't dismiss these out of hand.

NEW FOR THE NINETIES

1. The Parents' Charter means that your parents have a right to say which school they would prefer you to attend. Your local education authority will send your parents a jolly little booklet, listing all their state schools and saying how many pupils

they can admit to each. But be warned; they can still only take as many kids as they have room for and priority may go to those living closest or with brothers or sisters already there. Demand for the most popular school will be intense.

2. Individual schools produce glossy prospectuses, extolling the virtues of everything from their Baroque Music Group and Olympic-sized swimming pool to the number of clever clogs getting into university and the success of the Five-a-Side footie team. They also state the school's policies on all sorts of topics and are essential reading.

3. Some schools in certain areas are seeking – and getting – grammar school status. This can mean entrance exams and in–depth interviews with headteachers, in studies that smell of lavender polish and cough drops.

This all means that picking the right school for you takes forethought and planning. And while your parents have a lot of input, YOU need to get involved from day one.

WHAT YOUR PARENTS LOOK FOR

1. Something familiar. They like what they know. I suppose there are still parents who declare that you should go to their old school on the grounds that what was good enough for them is good enough for you, but thankfully they are a dying breed. Most mums and dads have your best interests at heart but being a parent, especially first time round, isn't easy and they worry about getting it right just as much, if not more, than you do. If they send you somewhere that they went to or at least a school like it, they feel they are in with a fighting chance. This is the sort of thing you might have to contend with.

What your father says: "Look what Denehurst School did for me."

What he means: "I know I'm not a company director or a star of stage and screen, but I haven't done too badly, have I? Really?"

What you may be tempted to say: "But Dad, you can't speak German, haven't grasped how to programme the video, and think CDT is a weedkiller for the lawn."

How to handle him: "Dad, you've done just great but I really think that a larger/smaller/more academic/less sporty school would suit me better."

What your mother says: "But the Willoughby twins love it at Quincote House!"

What she means: "I'm friends with their mother and it would be nice to know at least one other mum when you start."

What you may be tempted to say: "The fact that the Willoughby twins have half a gram of brain between them and ambitions to be checkout girls at Happy Buys does not immediately recommend the establishment to me."

How to handle her: "Oh I know, Mum, but then you are so much more broadminded and far-sighted than Mrs Willoughby, aren't you?"

The main purpose of all this friendly-speak is to

get the parents to understand that just because
your father had a whale of a time at the Hale and
Hearty Academy for Youth where potholing,
mountain scaling and cold showers formed an
integral part of everyday life, he can't assume that
the same regime will suit you. And just because
the girl who perms your mother's hair loved it at
Littleton Road School because they did Country
Dancing and the hall overlooked the Boys'
Grammar changing rooms does not mean that
you will be enraptured with the place.

2. They want the best for their children. Many parents have secret regrets about the things they never did, or the exams they never passed. They are very keen to make sure that you have every opportunity to do well in the world. So they are likely to look for a school with a strong academic record.

WHAT YOU LOOK FOR

1. At first you are probably only interested in going on to the school where the majority of your friends will be going. After all, a familiar face is very welcome in strange surroundings. But don't overlook any other possibilities just because you might not know anyone.

2. Would you be happiest at a single sex school or a co-ed? Do you like being among large numbers of people or would you be happiest in a small school? And what are your hopes for the future?

3. Some schools stream according to ability, others don't. Some like the competition of working to get into the A stream for Maths, others find it demoralising. Work out what is best

11

for you.

If all this seems daunting, let's make it easier. Still smiling and being hugely reasonable, sit the parents down with a freshly brewed pot of tea (always a good move), grab yourself a large bag of chocolate raisins and, using the following checklist, draw up the Short List.

DRAWING UP A SHORTLIST

1. WHAT DO YOU WANT OUT OF LIFE?

If you have an idea about what you want to do after school, that's great. Obviously if you have a mind to become a brain surgeon you need a school that excels in the Sciences. If, on the other hand, you see yourself as something of a Kenneth Branagh or Emma Thompson, Drama will be a pre-requisite.

If you haven't a clue about the future don't worry: most people don't. Just ask yourself questions about your current interests.

* Do you love leaping over hurdles, bashing hockey balls and spending the summer immersed in heavily chlorinated water?
Yes/No

* Is your idea of relaxation and fun playing the trumpet, setting up a jazz band or choreographing a new dance routine?
　Yes/No
　* Do you enjoy creative arts, such as pottery, design and handicrafts?
　Yes/No

Get the idea? If you love music, then a school with no orchestra and few opportunities to learn an instrument won't appeal. If you are keen on ceramics, look for somewhere with a decent CDT building and a kiln.

2. HAVE YOU KEPT YOUR OPTIONS OPEN?
Right now, while your knees are knocking at the thought of the first term, things like GCSEs and A levels seem light years away. But they come. Oh, believe me, they come. What you need to do now is make sure that the school you choose has plenty of subjects on offer, both at GCSE and A level. There is nothing more frustrating than deciding you want to combine English, Theatre Studies and Maths at A level, only to find your school doesn't mix Arts and Sciences.

SO
* Check out what subjects are on offer, at what

levels and in what combinations.
* Find out whether there are any plans to add
to, or worse, drop, any subjects.

* What non-examined subjects are on offer?
The good news is you do actually have things like
Current Affairs, Environmental Studies and so
on which are not part of the public exam system
but which add a lot to your understanding of Life
in the World Today.

3. WHAT IS YOUR SCENE?

Would you prefer to be part of a huge school or
be happier in a smaller one? Remember to think
about the facilities on offer in a big school and
balance those with the intimacy of one with fewer
pupils.

What about the sexes? I said The Sexes, not sex.
Are you and your parents looking for a single-sex
school (in which case the choice is usually limited
to one state school in each area) or a
co-educational establishment? You will hear all
sorts of arguments offered in favour of both and
in the end, you have to decide.

Arguments you will hear from people in favour of

single–sex schools:
*   Pupils concentrate more on their work and
less on attracting the opposite sex.
*   Girls are more intimidated academically in
subjects like Maths and Science when they are in
direct competition with boys.
*   Discipline is better when there are fewer
conflicts of interest.
*   Boys and girls ARE different and should be
taught differently.

*Arguments you will hear from people who are against
single–sex schools:*
*   School prepares you for the Real World. Men
and women live together in the real world, so
they should start learning the art right now.
*   Girls and boys are different and challenge
each other academically.
*   If boys and girls are together all the time at
school, they grow up as friends in a less intense
environment.

4. ARE YOU BEING PRACTICAL?
It is worth thinking about how you are going to
get to and from this seat of academia.
   Does the journey involve two buses and a half
mile walk? If so, this may seem OK in summer

but in early February with two feet of snow on the ground and a biting wind it may not resemble fun. And when you get involved in extra–curricular activities (assuming the school has resisted government cuts and still has them) you don't want to be walking home in the dark. The parents might fetch you once in a while, but the novelty of turning out twice a week in the middle of EastEnders tends to wear off.

Chapter Two
THE VISIT

And so to the visit. You must visit the school before your parents form any set ideas. In the set ideas department, parents are hard to shift once their minds are made up.

RULES FOR YOUR PARENTS

1. While they cast a critical eye over schools and school teachers, the teachers will be putting them under scrutiny as well. Indeed, many a staff coffee break is enlivened with tales of Craig Larkin's mother who tested the temperature of the water in the shower block or Amy Cosgrove's father who wanted to make a man of her. Parents should never say anything which might make their child look a fool.

2. Try to discourage your mother from dressing up as if she is about to attend a Buckingham Palace Garden Party. (Mothers like to "make a

STAYING COOL - SURVIVING SCHOOL

good impression" with teachers if only to prove
that your formative years have been in good
hands.) Likewise, fathers often under-dress to the
point of appearing in gardening sweaters with
fertiliser stains on the shoulder, white socks with
brown shoes, or their disreputable golfing cap.

3. If your parents have a tendency to talk about
you as if you were invisible, tactfully request that
they include you in the conversation. After all,
who is it who is going to be ensconced in the
school for the next five years?

Rules For You

1. Just as you want your parents to look passably
presentable, so they would appreciate it if you did
not wear the jeans with the holes in the knees,
T-shirts with rude slogans or trainers with
flapping soles. Like it or not, first impressions
count and you might as well do what you can to
look good.

2. It may be that you think the whole exercise is
pointless, or are inwardly sulking because you had
to put a skirt on, but try not to look too morose.
If you do, your parents will become even more

anxious, and quite possibly stop your pocket
money and the Head will have you labelled as
"potentially difficult" even before you have seen
the Science block. Much better to look interested,
smile frequently and utter the odd coherent
sentence. Get it to a fine art and the parents will
be so impressed they might be persuaded to stop
off for a new pair of Reeboks on the way home.

ASSESSING THE SCHOOL

The name of the game is Check It All Out. To
help you make sense of the whole shenanigan, fill
in the check-lists that follow to keep tabs on how
the school rates.

1. *THE HEAD*. The Head of any school, large or
small, is instrumental in creating the atmosphere
in which you will be spending the greater part of
your time for the next few years. Select him or her
with the utmost care.
a)   Did s/he:
i)   talk only to your parents and ignore you?
ii)   mutter the odd word at you but never look
you in the eye?
iii)   chat in a natural and friendly manner and
involve you in the conversation?

b) Did s/he:

(i) refer to you as "boy" or "girl"?

(ii) ask your name three times and then call you Alison instead of Alice or Gareth instead of Gary?

(iii) call you by your name as soon as you arrived?

COME HERE, GIRL ! ... ER ... BOY?

c) When other pupils passed and said, "Good morning," to the Head did s/he:

(i) nod vaguely in their direction?

(ii) say "Good morning um...er"

(iii)   reply cheerfully, "Good morning, Samantha/Jason/Peregrine and is your foot/ hamster/grandmother feeling better this morning?"

d) Did the Head listen carefully to all your parents had to say and then:
(i)   stand up and terminate the interview?
(ii)   call for coffee and start discussing the cricket team's success?
(iii)   ask you how you felt about the school, the curriculum, what your interests were and whether you liked badminton?

ANSWERS:
a)
(i)   0 points. If s/he ignores you this early on, it bodes ill for the coming years.
(ii)   2 points. While accepting that s/he may have a bit of grit in her/his eye or have lost her/ his contact lenses, lack of eye contact shows a certain uneasiness.
(iii)   5 points. Great. S/he acknowledges your presence and your worth as a person.

b)
(i)   0 points. You have a name and anyone with a modicum of respect for humanity would use it.

Teachers who need to impose their authority by demeaning others are not worth knowing.
(ii)   2 points. S/he may be hard of hearing, but, s/he may just not have bothered to listen.
(iii)   5 points. All s/he had to do was glance at the application letter or the appointment diary and check before letting you in.

c)
(i)   2 points. At least s/he acknowledged them.
(ii)   5 points. At least s/he said something.
(iii)   10 points. This is your man/woman. Some people say that in a big school it is impossible to learn everyone's first name. Wrong. I know three head-teachers who do it every year.

d)
(i)   2 points. S/he could be bursting to go to the loo or have an appointment with the Head of French but s/he should have planned enough time for you too.
(ii)   3 points. S/he is trying to be sociable but still forgetting you.
(iii)   10 points. Spot on. S/he knows that you need to ask questions and give opinions and s/he has allowed time for you to have your say.

SCORE
4-9 points. Forget it.
10-20 points. Has potential but needs working on.
21 and over. As near to ideal as you'll get.

2. THE TEACHERS

During your conducted tour of the school, you will visit various classrooms while lessons are in progress. Everything that applied to the Head is equally applicable to teachers. In addition, give plus points to teachers who:

*   Crack a joke, however feeble.
*   Praise their class in front of your parents.
*   Are moving around the classroom helping out, rather than sitting aloof at the front (unless it is test time).

Beware of those who:

*   Look thoroughly bored with the whole exercise.
*   Make snide remarks along the lines of, "Well, we are supposed to be working, Mr Palmer, but as you can see by looking at this bunch of morons, we are not." A sense of humour is essential in a teacher; hurtful sarcasm is not.

3. THE CLASSROOMS

What with all the cutbacks and the recession and the cost of gloss paint, some classrooms today would make authentic sets for a reconstruction of life at Colditz. How can anyone be expected to get

to grips with the finer points of the Civil War
when seated at a wobbly table on holey linoleum
with a force 10 gale blowing through an ill-fitting
windowframe?

Plus points to look for:

*   Cheerful posters covering the walls.
*   Well-stocked bookshelves – never mind if the
books are a bit tatty, it is better than nothing and
at least well-thumbed books have been read.
*   Plenty of pot plants – good for the vibes and
anything that is still alive gives you hope.
*   A moderately good supply of equipment –
one computer between 38 is not appropriate.

4. THE CAFETERIA/CANTEEN/DINING HALL

It is enormously difficult to assess how good or
bad the food is at any school before you actually
get there. Interviews and visits do not include
lunch and if they did, your parents would
probably get the Chicken Chasseur and Fruits in
Brandy kept for governors, the mayor and People
Who Might Donate a Sports Hall. You lot get
stew and solidified dumplings, rice pudding
complete with weatherproof skin, and flapjack
that doubles as a substitute for reinforced
concrete.

25

CANTEEN CHECK-LIST

i) Is there an all-pervading smell of boiled cabbage?

ii) Is there an all-pervading smell of bleach which has been used in a desperate attempt to get rid of the all-pervading smell of boiled cabbage?

iii) Is there a menu? If so, does it have dishes to suit vegetarians and members of ethnic minorities?

iv) Are there any decomposing lumps of food stuck under the chairs by desperate third formers?

v) Are the water jugs chipped? Caterers say that nowadays you have plastic jugs and they can't chip. After three months with the fifth form Rugby Lunch Club they can.

vi) Are the floorboards free of vomit stains?

If you get the chance to ask other kids what the food is like, be prepared to make allowances for the answers. Few pupils admit to liking school food. Don't listen to the Head - s/he may wax lyrical about the joys of the minced beef and onion pie but you can bet s/he will be in the staff-room with a smoked salmon sandwich out of Marks and Spencer.

5. THE GROUNDS

If your prospective school has playing fields and
tennis courts on site, so much the better. In inner
city areas you may have to pile on to a coach and
drive for three miles to play 30 minutes' hockey,
which is a bit of a hassle but sometimes cannot
be avoided. But do make sure there is some sort
of sports facility on the spot – a gym, sports hall
or swimming pool, or at least somewhere to play
a quick game of softball during the lunch hour. If
there is nothing, there is nowhere to let off steam
and when you are feeling fed up, premenstrual or
just bursting with energy, there is nothing worse
than having no excuse to hit something very hard.

6. *THE SICK BAY*

Even if you eat high-fibre muesli three times a day, run round the block on the hour, and bath in geranium oil, there will come a time during your school career when, in the middle of Maths, you suddenly find your stomach has taken leave of gravity or your body has begun to erupt into countless livid purple spots. On such occasions, you will be sent to the Sick Room. We shall discuss the joys of this haven of isolation later, but do check it out for essentials. I am afraid grey serge blankets still appear to reign supreme – perhaps they got a job lot at the end of the Crimean War – but make sure that the room looks moderately cheerful, has a television, a day room area for those who are poorly but not moribund and something to do to take your mind off your headache/shattered kneecap/wasp sting.

THINGS YOU SHOULD FIND OUT — BUT PROBABLY WON'T TILL YOU GET THERE

1. *SCHOOL RULES*

Every school has rules. Every school needs rules. That said, there are some rules which are essential and should be adhered to to the letter and others which seem a bit pointless. A few are ludicrous .

28

GOOD RULES

School uniform shall be worn at all times. Once a school has decided to adopt a uniform, it's pretty obvious they want you to wear it. And your parents, having forked out large sums of money to clothe you in brown and orange, are not likely to be happy if you slink off to school in jeans. *Solution:* Grin and bear it and wait till the sixth form when you can wear what you like.

Pupils going into town in their lunch hour shall go in groups of not less than three. You think that's crazy? Think on. There is safety in numbers. It would be great if every town centre was a haven of serenity and security but they aren't. If something goes wrong, one person stays with the victim, the other goes for help. Common sense, really. *Solution:* Be thankful people care.

Homework shall be handed in on due date. In that big wide world that parents and teachers go on about, deadlines count. Bosses aren't very keen on staff who say, "Sorry, Mr Threadgold, I would have had the accounts ready by today but I went bowling and forgot." So teachers train you to set yourself a schedule and stick to it.

If you have a really valid excuse, like illness,

the arrival of long lost Cousin Mirabelle from
Chile or a power cut, they will make exceptions.
Watching TV, dancing the night away at Ritzies
and losing the essay on the bus don't qualify.
Solution: Keep a notebook with deadlines marked
in red.

All pupils shall register at the start of the day.
Common sense. In case of fire, flood or other
disaster, they need to know just who is and who
is not in school.

DOTTY RULES
*Boys and girls shall maintain a distance of six inches
apart at all times.* Still written in the Rules and
Regulations list of one school. Totally
unenforceable so why have it? And what is so
magical about six inches? An example of school
dogma at its most ridiculous.

No make-up shall be worn at any time. Out-of-
date rule. Probably valid in the Fifties when
make-up denoted Girls of Loose Morals, but less
realistic in the Nineties when sheer make-ups are
all the rage. A better ruling would be "Light
unobtrusive make-up may be worn by girls in the
fifth form and above."

No jewellery, with the exception of wrist-watches, shall be worn. If you have pierced ears, you have to wear studs or the holes close up. Some ethnic communities wear jewellery by tradition and to denote status. Again "Jewellery should only be worn in moderation" would be better.

CLANK   CLANK

JINGLE

2. PUNISHMENTS
Detentions — Range from writing essays like "Silence is Golden" for people caught talking in class to cleaning the cups or revamping the library catalogue.

31

Menial tasks — Anything from cleaning out the test tubes in the chemistry lab to covering books in the library. The idea of these tasks is to bore you into being good next time.

Removal of privileges – This one usually works. If you have waited three years for the privilege of being allowed to use the Common Room and make toasted sandwiches for lunch, and then you find yourself banished back to the canteen with the first-years, you are unlikely to make the same mistake twice. Drawback – some schools are pretty thin in the privilege department and what you don't have can't be taken away.

Suspension — This is only for serious offences – smoking on school premises, caught in possession of alcohol, bullying, stealing. And frankly, under those circumstances, you deserve all you get.

Expulsion — This is the last resort. If you have been caught with drugs you will be expelled. Don't be that stupid.

THE FINAL DECISION

So – you've decided this school will do OK. Let the parents think it was their idea. It's no skin off your nose and it keeps their egos up. Of course, if you like the school and they are still hesitating, you need to employ tact. Your best line is something like, "I really feel I could work and give of my best there." This appeals to their inner desires to have an achieving child. If it is near your own home, point out the ease of travel. If all else fails, go quiet and pop a couple of glistening tears in the eyes. It usually works.

Chapter Three
THE ONE-TO-ONE WITH THE HEAD

"Say nothing good of yourself, you will be distrusted: say nothing bad of yourself, you will be taken at your word."
(Joseph Roux, French priest and writer)

With all the changes in education, more and more schools are in a position to choose who they take and who they don't. Some, like private schools, have The Entrance Exam. Your parents will drive themselves demented over this and they are not even taking the wretched thing. They will in all probability grill you with spelling tests, mental arithmetic marathons and general knowledge inquisitions. They will tell you to sit up straight, act your age, write neatly, remember to use a few commas and go on at length about this being a great opportunity and not to let it slip through your fingers.

Try not to let all this intensity get to you: just do your best (which sounds very trite and corny but is in fact all you can do, and anyway they want to know if you have the right idea, not if you are perfect at getting the right answer every time).

What many schools do have is a one-to-one chat with the Head. They don't call it an interview, but that's what it is really. There is an art to interviews. For years, your parents have been telling you to tell the truth, the whole truth and nothing but the truth. Well, in your school interview, I humbly suggest you modify the truth. Like this:

Question: *WHAT DID YOU DO IN THE SUMMER HOLIDAYS?*
Truthful answer: Lounged around watching Neighbours and eating popcorn; eyed up the talent in Benidorm and spent all my money in the video arcades.
Improved answer: Had a wonderful time in Spain integrating with the local life and improving my Spanish. (Well, you learned how to say "Get orf" in Alicantese, didn't you?)

Question: *WHAT CONTRIBUTION DO YOU THINK YOU COULD MAKE TO THE LIFE OF THE SCHOOL?*
Truthful answer: I do a good line in caricatures, can make stink bombs at the drop of a hat and am great at thinking up scams for April Fool's

Day.
Improved answer: I enjoy art in all its forms, would like to establish an Alternative Science Club and am interested in farce.

Question: *WHY DO YOU WANT TO COME TO HIGHFIELD GRAMMAR?*
Truthful answer: I am not fussed either way – it's the parents who are in a frenzy about it.
Improved answer: Because I want to learn as much as possible in order to have a successful career. (At this point you will want to vomit at your own tweeness but don't worry, him or her in the leather armchair will be well impressed. They like a few up-and-coming Captains of Industry in the school.)

Question: *WHAT BOOKS HAVE YOU BEEN READING RECENTLY?*
Truthful answer: This month's issue of Just 17 and Love in the Laundrette.
Improved answer: (Fast thinking needed for this one – choose something erudite you have seen adapted on telly.) Tale of Two Cities, Great Expectations, The Borrowers.

Question: *WHAT DID YOU PARTICULARLY ENJOY ABOUT THE BOOK?*

Truthful answer: Oh cripes I didn't really read it I only saw it on telly.

Improved answer: The wonderful characterisation, fast-moving plot and use of language. (Covers most books fit for adaptation on telly and impresses the Head with your grasp of English.)

Question: *WHAT DO YOU DO IN YOUR SPARE TIME?*

Truthful answer: Not a lot.

Improved answer: Reading (makes you sound intelligent), walking (they cannot prove you don't), photography (well you took a picture of a friend apple-bobbing last Hallowe'en). Warning: it's a bit risky to admit to sporting interests unless you really are keen. They tend to remember and rope you into teams and then you wish you had shut up.

Chapter Four
MAKING YOUR SCHOOL UNIFORM BEARABLE
(anyone who doesn't have to wear one, thank your lucky stars and skip this chapter)

"You look rather rash my dear – your colours don't quite match your face."
(Daisy Ashford in *The Young Visitors*)

FACT: Many schools have uniform and insist on your wearing it.
FACT: Most school uniforms appear to have been designed by colour-blind frumps with about as much sense of style as a Patagonian tentmaker.
FACT: School uniforms come in the most ghastly of colours – purple, mustard, sludge and puce to name but a few.
FACT: Every garment takes on a life of its own after one whirl in the washing machine.

BUT: All is not lost.

While head-teachers enthuse until they are pink about the gills that school uniform is a great leveller and means that everyone looks the same, you have only to cast an eye round any school playground to realise this is not true. Oh sure, it means that even though Samantha Trussington's father is something big in textiles and can afford to buy her designer gear, she doesn't look any different from Tom Russell whose father ran off with a petrol pump attendant and left his mum to clothe, feed and generally nurture five kids and a Jack Russell terrier.

The difference lies in how people deal with their uniform. You need to know the tricks of the trade.

SKIRTS:
These tend to be grey, slime, maroon or navy, be made of the sort of fabric that goes shiny within ten days, and have about as much shape as a bin liner. Shorten them to anything approaching a fashionable length and the side seams bulge, giving you the appearance of a badly wrapped Easter egg. Even if you do manage to convert them into mini skirts, some bright spark in the staffroom will unearth an antiquated rule about knees being covered at all times.

WRONG THING TO DO: Argue, shout, shorten them to mid knicker length anyway and say to hell with the lot of you.

RIGHT THING TO DO: Shorten them by about a half inch a fortnight and tell the teachers you are on vitamin supplements and growing very fast and your mum is saving the Child Benefit for a new skirt. Damp eyes help. You will get a pat on the shoulder, be told not to overdo things and no more will be said.

More and more schools are allowing skirts from chain stores and these are much more shapely and well made.

BLAZERS:
Some schools still insist on this somewhat archaic garment. You can see their point – they do look very smart and suit all shapes and sizes. The parents will acquire the largest possible size available, and at £70 a throw who can blame them? The trouble with new blazers is that they look so new. The sleeves tend to engulf your fingertips and the braid stuff round the edge looks like a curtain tie-back.

WRONG THING TO DO: Wash it in hopes it will shrink. Blazers don't wash – they come out looking like damp felt and about the right size for an anorexic Sindy doll.

RIGHT THING TO DO: Try to persuade Mother to shorten the sleeves, then the rest looks better. One day, casually drop said blazer in a small but preferably stagnant puddle; parental shrieking and slamming of doors will follow but after much sponging down and brushing the offending garment will have lost that pristine look. Chalk dust rubbed into the elbows is the next step – but I would wait a couple of days for that one.

SHIRTS:
If you are lucky your school will settle for white shirts and no more said. If you are not, they will

42

have decided that girls are to wear lime and cream striped happenings that make the Third Year look like a group of ice lollies. Collars on school uniform shirts never sit right: no matter what shape your neck they curl up at the edges or crinkle round your hairline.

WRONG THING TO DO: Starch the collar. You come out in a pink rash and start turning blue because you can't breathe.

RIGHT THING TO DO: Wear a high-necked sweater or leave the top button undone and when reprimanded for such indecency explain that you were feeling faint.

TIES:
Boys and girls alike often wear these, which is fine if they are understated little numbers and not so fine if they have weird crests/pigeon-toed eagles/Latin mottoes on them. Some girls' schools have gone totally bananas and exchanged ties for velvet ribbons which get thrown in the Heavy Soil wash and come out looking like faded shoelaces. Ties are rather ridiculous garments, guaranteed to attract gravy stains, ink blots, Tipp-Ex blotches and other unmentionables but they do come in useful as temporary fanbelts or handles for school bags.

GAMES KIT:

The last kit list I read insisted on two pairs of trainers. Unless you have four feet, ignore this before your parents throw a whoopsie and the bank forecloses. However, two sports shirts are a good idea if you have the average mother. They are prone from time to time (usually once a month) to hurl bright red pyjamas into the same wash as pure white games shirts and who wants to hurtle round the tennis court in pink? Track suits are usually insisted on but sadly in the school colours and totally shapeless.

When your parents see the price of football kit, tennis racquets, hockey sticks and cricket bats they will utter some very rude words (which you are forbidden even to think). The anger masks a genuine fear of their bank manager and a desire to do the right thing.

WRONG THING TO DO: Insist that you have everything brand new and have it now.

RIGHT THING TO DO: Suggest you have the tennis racquet for your birthday or borrow a mate's outgrown footie boots for a month or so. Your parents will be grateful and you will come up smelling of roses.

ACCESSORIES:
The school bag – it needs to be huge, sturdy, spongeable and individualised in some way. There is nothing more annoying than grabbing your bag, rushing for the bus and arriving home to find you've got Toby Andrew's bag which contains nothing but running shoes and a half-eaten peanut butter sandwich.

Reinforced handles come in handy by the Fifth Year when you are humping the contents of three libraries around with you, and a side pocket for essentials like bus passes, door keys and locker keys helps keep you organised.

Maths sets – Get the kind that come in a tin – those plastic zip–up jobs look great till the zip breaks, the plastic tears and you lose your set–square down a drain.

Calculators – Allowed these days which is good news. Your father will mutter something about having to do it the proper way in his day, but you can bet he will be borrowing it to work out how much he won on the Grand National.

Chapter Five
THE FIRST WEEK

"The schoolboy, with his satchel and shining morning face, creeping like snail, unwillingly to school."

(William Shakespeare)

The first few days anywhere new can be pretty nerve-racking. Your father will doubtless slap you on the back at the breakfast table, causing you to choke violently on your Wheatyloops, and boom, "You'll have a great time, what on earth are you worrying about?" but you can bet your life that on his first day as Deputy Sales Manager Eastern Region (Area 3) he was so uptight that he put the cat in the fridge and the milk in the garden. There are, however, ways of easing the trauma.

COMMON PROBLEMS IN WEEK ONE

1. COPING WITH THE NEW BUILDING

The switch from primary school to secondary
school is a big one. There is more of everything
and it is all in different places. Some schools give
new kids a plan of the layout, which makes
getting from PE in the gym to Biology in the lab a
lot easier. Just remember that everyone was new
once and if you get lost, ask. Teachers will make
allowances at least for the first week and you will
be surprised at how quickly you find your way
around.

2. BACK TO THE BOTTOM OF THE HEAP

When you were in the top year at primary school
you probably got the chance to boss the little kids
a bit, sit on a separate table for lunch and get to
be prefect or games captain. Now it's back to
being a tiny cog in a big wheel and you may well
feel lost and insignificant to start with. It'll pass.
And for the first few weeks, it's best to just watch
and wait.

3. THE NEW TIMETABLE

In secondary school, you have different lessons in
different rooms with different teachers. You have

to remember where you are meant to be and to
ensure you have the right books with you at the
time. During the first week you will find yourself
chuffed to be in Room 8 for Geography – and
then discover that you have brought History of
our Times instead of Cloud Formations Book
Two. Tip: put a red sticky dot on Geography
books, a blue one on History and so on; great
when you are in a hurry (but make sure the book
is covered first).

49

4. APPEARANCE

You will have taken note of the advice on scruffing up your school uniform, assuming you have one, and spent hours in front of the mirror to ensure that you look just right – not too tidy, not a complete blob. If your mother has acted like thousands of her kind and insisted on shiny new shoes, spend the time waiting for the bus spinning round on your toes to scuff shoes slightly (only slightly or your mother may well throw a whoopsie and end up in the Overnight Psychiatric Unit at the General which won't do the family credibility a lot of good). Make sure one shirt button is undone. You will be told to button it up as soon as you get there, but that should only serve to prove to everyone that you are a cool kid. That should do for starters.

MAKING FRIENDS

This is what everyone dreads. "Supposing no-one talks to me" is the worst worry of all as the school bus draws up at the bus stop. With a bit of luck some of your primary school friends will be going to the same school so there will be a few familiar faces. While it is terribly tempting to stick like limpets to people you know, and quite okay to do so for the first couple of days, it's a good idea to get to know other people as well. But to do this

with any degree of success you need to observe a
while. There are a lot of telltale signs that will
help you pick out those you want to cultivate and
those best avoided.

THE QUEEN BEES (or KING PINS)
"Well, hi there, I'm Stella, who are you?" This is
a typical introduction from the Potential Leader of
the Pack, the sort of embryo PR type who has no
qualms about anything – or so it seems. Oozing
self-confidence from every pore, they purport to
knoweverything about everybody and far from
exhibiting first –day nerves, usually end up as
Class Prefect, Person in Charge of Library Tickets
and Producer of the Class Play by the middle of
the first week. The male variety, the King Pins, are
somewhat more aggressive. They will assure
anyone with the time and inclination to listen
that they are going to carve a path through the
school, make people sit up and take notice and
change anything they don't like.
    WARNING: Queen Bees and King Pins tend
to ditch anyone who is not prepared to worship at
their throne, or dares to suggest that their way is
not necessarily the best. In short, they are only
happy when they are the centre of attention and
may well use other people for their own ends.
Handle with care.

HALE HENRY AND HEARTY HANNAH

Fortunately for the ongoing success of Great
Britain in the Olympic Games, Round the World
Yacht races and mountain conquering, there are a
large number of frightfully energetic,
health–conscious kids whose idea of bliss is to
charge around a muddy field wielding a hockey
stick or fall flat on their faces in a bed of nettles
while attempting to beat the school Cross
Country record. If you are one of these, then get
together with them early on and spend the next
five years dashing about at high speed and
developing your pectorals. If, however, you are of

the belief that if God had meant us to run he would have put spikes on our feet, take care. These types love to get everyone involved. They rush round whipping up teams for everything from Stoolball to Shuffleboard, beg the Games Staff to start an after-school aerobics class and invite you round to their place for supper, only to end up suggesting a quick game of badminton when you would rather be watching Drop the Dead Donkey. They cannot imagine why anyone would bribe their mother to write an Off Games Note and frequently go around looking a trifle grubby on account of the mudstained kneecap acquired while vaulting a five-barred gate on the way to Maths.

TIMID TARA AND NERVOUS NEIL

Not everyone takes on the challenge of a new school with flair and aplomb. For many it is fraught with enough anxiety to reduce them to quivering, tearful heaps. Before you criticise and call them wimps, pause a moment and think why. Many of these kids have parents back home who are insisting that they come out with straight As or end up as Captain of Football or Head Girl. Some may be faced with pretty traumatic home lives about which, at this stage at least, you know nothing. Some just may find the idea of chatting to 25 total strangers overwhelming and who can blame them? Of course, the sad thing is that many of these less ebullient souls are so worried about making the right impression or just merging into the background that they fail to do either. These are the types who drop the pile of exercise books they have been asked to distribute around the class on day one, or spill the soup as they timidly make their way from the self-service cafeteria to a corner table. Be friendly and make them feel needed. You might be amazed that a potentially very good friend is hiding underneath the frightened exterior.

THE BRAINBOXES – CHARLOTTE CLEVER CLOGS AND BRILLIANT BENEDICT

These are the kids for whom two hours of differential calculus is sheer joy and whose idea of a cushy number is a four page essay on the causes of the French Revolution. They can't help being brilliant any more than you can help having a wart on your index finger. It's in their genes. The problem comes when they flaunt their intelligence morning, noon and night. "It's so easy" they yawn as they see you struggling to discover why x=y squared. "God, haven't you done that French essay yet?" they sneer as you battle with Madame Jolie's vacances en Angleterre. The more amenable brainboxes will offer to do it for you, but be warned. Your teacher is not daft and it is unlikely that she will believe that someone who only yesterday got 4 out of 20 for a French test, is suddenly writing with all the skill and flair of Voltaire. The best hope is that you can make friends with someone clever enough and kind enough to point you in the right direction and avoid your making some of your worst mistakes.

THE CHIPPENDALE

These are the boys who really fancy themselves as macho men. Muscle flexing and posing is a way of life with them and they imagine that every female is about to swoon away at the sight of their rippling flesh and every male is dying of envy over their pectorals. They walk with an exaggerated swagger, wear open-necked shirts and chew a lot. They flaunt their burgeoning masculinity all day till everyone is bored sick with them. Funny thing is, ask them to lift a couple of bookcases for you and suddenly they don't want to put their ripples at risk.

CINDY – Mind my nails – CHARMER

This is a female version of the above, liable to suffer from wrist injuries caused by the excessive flicking of hair over right shoulder, or cracked lips

brought on by continuous pouting. Far more interested in plucking her eyebrows or painting her nails than learning anything, she is convinced that because she is pretty the world owes her a living and she is destined for the catwalks of Paris and Milan. Doesn't like Games in case she breaks a nail, hates Science because it's smelly and skives off swimming in case her fake tan washes off. Harmless, but can be jolly aggravating if you are spending two evenings a week bleaching your upper lip and never eat Chockywheats because of your buttocks.

THE VOLUNTEERS

"Please, Miss, I'll do it, Miss, please Miss!". This is the constant cry of the Noble, Self–Effacing and I'm So Good Aren't I, Miss, Volunteers. Usually female, they rush around piling up chairs, watering rubber plants and ministering to ailing classmates. Drawing up lists and collecting funds is their idea of heaven and they follow members of staff around the school with expressions of adulation on their intense little faces. They can be sickeningly irritating until you realise that they are desperate to please and yearn for affection which they are just possibly not finding anywhere else. The big danger with the Volunteers is that they are so desperate for friends that it makes them easy prey to the Bullies (see below). No one, anywhere, ever deserves to be bullied and even if you think the Volunteer types are pretty daft, try to see things through their eyes. Suggest that they pause for ten minutes, in between counting out lunch tickets and collecting for Oxfam, and have a coffee; what they really want is someone who needs them. These types can become pretty clingy so don't go overboard to start with.

THE BULLIES

These are the worst type of kid anywhere. They use their own strength to play on other people's weaknesses and can make the lives of their victims sheer hell. Basically they are cowards who can only feel at ease with themselves when they are making someone else's life a misery. There is never any good reason for bullying. If you ever see anyone being bullied, make it your business to tell someone in authority at once. Not tomorrow, not later today. NOW. Tomorrow may be too late.

If it is *you* that is being bullied, you must also tell someone at once. The bullies may say they will get you for it, but they won't be allowed to if you go straight to the top. Tell the Head, tell your class teacher, tell the police if necessary. But don't let them get a hold over you. If you want more advice, read *Don't Pick On Me* (Piccadilly Press, £5.99) – it's a great book and stops you feeling that no-one out there understands. But DO something. Your life and your peace of mind are too precious to be threatened by anyone.

THE COOL TRENDIES

These are the guys and girls who wear the hip outfits with that certain style that is always The Look of the Moment. Never mind *in* fashion; they *make* the fashion. They are totally on top of every situation, set the trends for the rest of the school and appear to lick every problem into place by breaktime. You are bound to envy them but don't; the trouble with their lifestyle is that it is very transient. They have to keep thinking up new scams to keep ahead. Exhausting.

THE MAJORITY

Having listed all the quirks of kids above, you may wonder if you will find anyone just like you. In fact, the vast majority are thoroughly ordinary, normal everyday types who have their good days, bad days and bored days. Whatever you may think as you stand, knees-a-tremble, in line for your first Assembly, they all have their worries as well, be they difficult parents, BO or sticking out teeth. Give them all a chance and you will end up with a whole clutch of new friends.

UNDERSTANDING THE TEACHERS

*"I owe a lot to my teachers and mean to pay them
back some day."*
(Stephen Leacock)

Henry B Adams (who you might like to know, in
order to impress your teacher one day, was an
American historian) once said "A teacher affects
eternity." By which he meant get a good one and
what you learn lasts a lifetime; get a bad one and
s/he can put you off for life. You will soon
discover that every school has its brilliant
teachers, its not–so–sparkling ones and its
despots. Rather like life, really.

THE MOTHERLY TYPE

This is one of the best sort of teachers you can
get. She is friendly, unshockable and down–to–
earth. Sometimes this is because she is a mum
herself; often it's just because she actually likes
kids a lot. Whatever her subject, she will be aware
that not everyone will enjoy it, unlike some
members of staff who take it as a personal affront
if you do not view their speciality as the highlight
of your day.
BUT BE WARNED: Don't make the mistake of
thinking that she is a soft touch. She is adept at

handling the subversive and the downright
awkward and she can show her core of steel at the
most surprising times. This is the type who, with
a broad smile on her face, will say, "Well now,
Philip, as you are so quick with the backchat I
think I might give you the honour of writing a
pilot sitcom for the Fourth Year Drama Group.
I'll have it on my desk by 8.30 tomorrow
morning. How kind."

How to get on the right side of The Motherly Type:
Be yourself. She cannot stand airs and graces,
deception or pretence. If you don't understand,
say so. If you need help, ask. Provided you try,
she will like you.

THE ACADEMIC *(also known as THE TOTALLY VAGUE)*

You might be forgiven for thinking that in order to be A Teacher you have to be very with-it. Wrong. A lot of teachers, particularly male ones of advancing years, appear to drift through life in a fog of geniality, nodding absent-mindedly at passers-by and viewing the world with the benign expression of a well-fed ox. This apparent disregard for the world about them stems from an Overactive Intellect. After all, when your mind is full of differential calculus or the Sacking of Rome, you don't have a lot of time left to become au fait with the goings-on in Summer Bay. The only time these types spring into life is when they are in full flood about their own subject – then there is no stopping them. Sometimes they forget to set prep – but make up for it by giving you twice as much the following week.

BE WARNED: Some clever people find it hard to believe that not everyone understands what they are saying first time round. If you don't understand what he is saying because he is using words of more than two syllables or mumbling into the blackboard, say so. He may be an academic, but he doesn't have access to a crystal ball and if you stay quiet, he will simply assume that you are following the lesson. Which could prove nasty when the time comes for the exams.

How to get on the right side of The Vague Academic: once in a while, say, "Gosh, sir, that IS interesting." (He will be so amazed and chuffed that he will overlook your shortcomings for at least a week afterwards.)

Show an interest in something. It frankly doesn't matter what, and certainly it won't be held against you if it is not his subject. He just believes that everyone needs a Passion in order to survive. Find one and tell him about it and you have an ally.

THE WORRIER

Usually female, can be most irritating but have their uses. They worry that you might be worried because you cannot cope with the Hanoverians; they fret themselves silly about whether Jemima Higgins is sitting in a draught from the skylight and get terribly upset when a crowd of fifth form boys sings rugby songs under the staffroom window. Should a parent fail to wave to her in the shopping centre on a Saturday, she panics that she has offended someone and if asked to show parents of a prospective pupil around the school, her nervous twitch coupled with hot flush gives her the appearance of a budgie after a workout.

PLUS POINTS Should you need Band-Aids, painkillers, a polythene bag, tomorrow's weather forecast or six tapes of How to Pass Exams Without Making Yourself Ill she will have them at the ready. Her obsession with things going wrong means she carries the remedies around with her at all times. And she's a good bet for getting you out of things. Tell her you have a headache and she will assume it must be a brain tumour and send you home to Mother.

BE WARNED: Worriers tend to chat to their colleagues in the staffroom, if only to unload their anxieties. So don't try your luck too much or you might cop it from another teacher for taking advantage of her caring nature.

How to get on the right side of The Worrier: tell her that since she taught you things have been much easier. She will be so thrilled that she might even forget to worry for a bit. Until tomorrow, when she will grab you by the shoulder and say, "Now I'm a bit worried that because you understand the subject, you will sit back and stop working." There is no pleasing some people.

THE HOARDER

This chap, often a crusty bachelor who has been at the school since the Boer War, is not so much concerned with the success of your education as with the cost of getting you there. This is the chap who keeps jam jars full of pencil stubs on his desk top, and refuses to hand out fresh chalk for the blackboard until the current piece is a mere blackened stub. He has you writing, not only on both sides of the paper, but up the margins as well. His clothes reflect his hatred of parting with hard cash; baggy trousers from an old suit, coupled with a mustard-coloured, hand knitted sweater given to him by Aunt Edna and a raincoat acquired at the Help the Aged shop because the aged didn't want it.

BE WARNED: Hoarders hate waste. So don't let him see you throwing away a used envelope or turning an elastic band into a catapult or you will be spending break time melting down soap ends for the staff loo.

How to get on the right side of The Hoarder: Collect all the elastic bands that the postman drops and hand them to The Hoarder before Assembly. He will greet the gift as you or I would welcome a large cheque from the grandparents.

THE ENTHUSIAST
Jolly chaps, these. No matter whether their particular joy is the collecting of fossils or the rendering of an oratorio, their sheer joy infects everyone, which makes them ideal producers of

school plays, organisers of trips abroad and ralliers of volunteers for the Bring and Buy Sale. They walk amazingly quickly because they are so keen to get where they are going, show an interest in absolutely everything from the Meaning of Life to the structure of the custard at school lunch and are the mainstay of the after-school-activities. Trouble is, they simply cannot understand why everyone else does not find Lino Printing for Pleasure as riveting as they do and get very upset when they only find two First Years interested in Water Aerobics.

BE WARNED: Unless you are prepared to be roped in to organise the Hobbies Club, never make casual remarks about how you are building a model T Ford or how your dad enjoys making railway layouts.

How to get on the right side of The Enthusiast. Assure him that you think his idea for an after school Barbershop group is terrific but sadly you are already committed to three societies, two clubs and an arthritic grandmother after hours and just cannot fit him in. Look saddened. He will assume you are another Enthusiast but that someone else got there first.

THE DESPOT
This is the staff equivalent of the bully. They are

thankfully few and far between but they do exist. This is the sort of teacher who dishes out snide remarks and scathing comments at the drop of a hat and who revels in making kids feel small or stupid. This is in fact because the teacher has a vast inferiority complex – they probably wanted to be a brain surgeon and failed Chemistry.

BE WARNED: Just because you don't get on with someone doesn't make them a Despot. Before you make accusations, ensure that you have a case. Then don't bother about getting on the right side of them or fighting back. Just ask to drop that subject and then tell the Head, your parents and any other interested party why.

Chapter Six
STUDY, STUDY AND MORE STUDY

"His studies were pursued but never effectually overtaken."
(H.G. Wells)

POTENTIAL PITFALLS

1. THE TIMETABLE
This tells you what you will be doing, when you will be doing it and where. (It rarely tells you why.) One thing you will have to learn at secondary school is that every subject has a different teacher and is taught in a different room. Which means that in the course of the average week you will walk the equivalent of a mini–marathon, usually lugging a pile of books with you. Then when you get there, you discover it was the wrong pile. Every teacher thinks his or her subject is the only one that really matters. Hence it is no good at all telling Mr Bonner of History that you are late for his fascinating

dissertation on the Boer War because Mrs Supple wanted to chat about your failure to grasp the past participle. To him, History is all and that is that.

2. HOMEWORK

You get a lot more homework at secondary school than you ever did at primary, if indeed you had any at all. It comes every night and consists of rather more than twenty minutes spent drawing a map of your village or reading a couple of chapters of The Borrowers. The National Curriculum demands that you learn such niceties as when to use a comma and how to discover the length of time taken by eight men to mend five

holes in 38 metres of broken motorway. (If the
M25 is anything to go by, about two years.)

3. DEADLINES

Now you are at secondary school, you will be
expected to think for yourself. Hence if your
English teacher says she wants an essay in by
Friday lunchtime, she expects you to remember
that fact and won't remind you.

Just remember that even the subjects you don't
like that much have their uses.

4. GRADES

Now your work will be graded. Sometimes it's
done in percentages, but usually by letter. A is
mega brilliant and deserves a Big Mac and two
strawberry milkshakes, B– is pretty decent and
should keep the parents off your back for another
week, C is a mite worrying and suggests that more
time spent working and less playing Sonic the
Hedgehog might be helpful.

5. SUBJECTS

MATHEMATICS

FACT: Maths teachers are by and large not that
keen on fingers. By the time you get to secondary

school they like you to be able to work out sums without taking your shoes off to use your toes because the total comes to more than ten. Calculators are allowed and you will be shown lots of quick ways of working out boring things.

HANDY HINT: If you have any sense, you will use this new-found knowledge to ascertain whether your parents have been paying you pocket money without any regard to rising inflation. Using compound interest, work out that they owe you £35.56p and ask for it now. Then remind them that they were thrilled when the school said that it concentrated on the "application of mathematical principles to everyday situations."

ENGLISH
FACT: English teachers all look a little anxious these days, ever since the Education Minister woke up to the fact that the "It's the content that counts, spelling doesn't matter" approach has produced a nation that cannot even remember to put i before e except after c, let alone spell accommodate and rhododendron.

HANDY HINT: You will have to write essays, – anything from "My most embarrassing moment" to "Do we care enough for our planet?" The former is no bother – just observe the

parents for a weekend and inspiration will flow –
but for the latter you need to write a little more
than "Yes" or alternatively "No". Sunday
supplements are a good source of info, and odd
phrases such as "When listening to Radio 4's
magnificent 'World of Wonder' I noted that..."
convince them in the staffroom that they will
eventually be able to "make something of you".
Since your parents will be nagging you senseless
about giving your all, it might be worth
reminding your mama that you noted down her
actions on the day she drove into the bus stop
and that maybe it would make a nice feature
under the "Humour" section of the school
magazine. That should quieten her down for a
bit.

THEATRE STUDIES

FACT: Can be taken for GCSE but also as a non-examined option. Most schools put on a production at least once a year to which parents will come to bask in the glow of their offspring's thespian talents.

HANDY HINT: Don't hang back from volunteering for a role; it gives you a wonderful excuse for legalised showing off, wearing make-up and forgetting to take it off, and getting out of written homework in order to learn your lines. If prancing about on stage is not your scene, remember they need make-up artists, lighting technicians and stage designers. Something for everyone.

FRENCH

FACT: The ability to speak with tongues is not given to us all.

HANDY HINT: Despite this, French is one of the most useful subjects you will do. It's a living language and with barriers tumbling all over Europe, you will need to parle with foreigners. It is also worth persevering with this because of The French Trip about which we speak later on. French is also rather useful for impressing people next time you find yourself in Jean Paul's bistro – it's more fun learning how to say "Please bring me a large dish of coq au vin and a bottle of claret" than remembering how to recount that the house of my young friend Marie is burning to the ground in Chantilly.

HISTORY
FACT: Your enjoyment of this subject can be made or destroyed by the teacher. History teachers come in two varieties: truly inspired or totally expired. The inspired ones realise that half the pleasure of learning about the Black Death is to discover just what the symptoms were, how long the pus took to ooze out the sores and what they did with the bodies. The expired variety are often nearing retirement, obsessed with the financial policy of Henry VII (who was a boring tight-fisted so-and-so anyway). A good History teacher will take you off to Hampton Court and turn a blind eye while you run around the maze; a bad one will drone on for hours about Tudor architecture without actually showing you any.

HANDY HINT: History has its uses. When you are struggling with an essay for another subject, you can hurl in the odd historical reference and earn not only five more marks but the amazed respect of whichever teacher you have stunned with the breadth of your knowledge. For instance, in an essay about the environment in the nineties, you could say "Sadly, the site of the Battle of Naseby is now threatened by an encroaching four-lane motorway" or mention that the Roman form of underfloor heating was jolly kind to the ozone layer (even though they didn't know there was one). This is what is called Legalised Showing Off. Teachers love it.

GEOGRAPHY

FACT: This is one subject where you can get out and about. The best bits are the videos of volcanic eruptions, being allowed out of class to go up on the roof to measure rainfall (but you only get to do that in the first year) and trips to view oxbow lakes.

HANDY HINT: Most geography field trips by their very nature take place in bog-ridden, mosquito-infested swamps where your teacher will eulogise for hours on the flora and fauna and you will spend the whole time scratching and degunging your Reeboks.

One good thing about geography is that you need not worry too much about revising all those maps. By the time you have memorised the map of Europe, all the borders will have changed and you will have to start all over again.

COMPUTER STUDIES

FACT: People who can whizz in and out of computer programs without batting an eyelid stand a good chance of getting jobs in the future.

HANDY HINT: What you need to do is get your parents to understand that if you are to have any chance of doing well at this subject you simply MUST have a computer to practise on at home. Be sure at this point not to mention games. Let them think you are dedicated to evolving a program for calculating the gross national product for the next two centuries. If family funds forbid such an investment, make friends with kids who are happy to let you use theirs.

ANOTHER HANDY HINT: If you want to get out of lessons for a couple of days you could try saying you have RSI. This means Repetitive Strain Injury and comes from bashing the keyboard too much. There is a slight drawback: 45 minutes twice a week is unlikely to induce anything mildly repetitive except perhaps frustration because you would rather be playing Sonic 2 than charting the progress of soil erosion on the cricket pitch.

SCIENCE

FACT: Without a doubt, the world is made up of

two species of individual: those who understand and can do things scientific and those who can't.

HANDY HINT: Even if you turn out to be one of the "can'ts", Science will come in handy for dealing with your wardrobe. If you have a particularly grotty shirt that your mother insists has at least two more terms' wear in it, a short encounter with a drop of acid works wonders – but remove yourself from the shirt first.

Try to get some fun out of it. Chemistry is good when you are boiling things up or blowing things up and deadly when you have to work out why. Physics seems to be all about action and reaction and light and electricity. Can be quite useful when you want to rig up speakers and flashing lights in the garden shed for your girlfriend's birthday disco. Biology is all leaves and photosynthesis and DNA and chromosomes and is quite fun because you discover how your innards are working and why. Or why not, as the case may be.

CRAFT, DESIGN AND TECHNOLOGY

FACT: This covers metalwork, woodwork and other crafts but you won't get away with just making a coffee table or a garden gate. You have to know all about the materials you use, the different types of glue, the variety of veneers available. Indeed, you could end up refurnishing your bedroom on the strength of your new-found skills.

HANDY HINT: Try everything on offer in the first couple of years. You might find you have a skill you never knew about. After all, there isn't much opportunity to make a wrought-iron magazine rack at home.

ART AND CERAMICS
FACT: A great way to experiment with different mediums, get messy and give vent to your hidden creative talents. It's very therapeutic to knead a lump of clay when you have just had an hour of Applied Mathematics.

LATIN AND GREEK

FACT: These classical subjects still flourish in the public schools but are much less common in state schools, where the demands of the jolly old National Curriculum are killing them off. What with all the compulsory stuff, and the Business Studies and Art, the Classics don't get much of a look in.

HANDY HINT: Knowing a smattering of Latin helps when solving crossword puzzles and learning other languages. Of course, if you are of the school of thought that "Latin is a dead language, as dead as dead can be; it killed the ancient Romans and now it's killing me" you will be perfectly happy to forget it.

PHYSICAL EDUCATION

FACT: If you are the sort of person who believes that summers were made for stretching out in the sun with a good book, and winters for curling up in front of the fire with a good book, Games may not appeal.

FACT: If you see yourself as something of a Gabriella Sabatini with the tennis racquet or a Harvey Thorneycroft on the rugby pitch, you will probably enjoy games more than any other part of the week and be a favourite with Games Staff who are, without exception, fighting fit, ruddy-cheeked souls who love yelling at people to run faster/kick harder/get those knees up higher.

HANDY HINT: For the faint-hearted, it has to be said that there are ways to get out of Games. The obvious ones, ranging from verrucas (for swimming) to sprained ankles (for hockey and soccer) have been done to death and frankly don't wash any more, especially when you forget to limp ten minutes after assuring Miss Hurrah of Hathletics that you cannot put your foot to the ground without fainting clean away. Post-viral fatigue syndrome is a little gem but they will demand a Note; coughs come in handy if you start to splutter and gasp on the pitch and get sent off (do look mortified at having to miss the second half) and double vision, which cannot be proved either way, comes in useful on the odd occasion.

ANOTHER HANDY HINT: Games aren't that bad and it is a good idea to latch onto one sport that you think you could enjoy and try to get good at it. Rugby can be played later at university and in local clubs, and cricket goes on till you are in your dotage. Tennis is a great one because you don't need a huge team to play and you can have games with friends at weekends and in the holidays. Whatever you play, just think of all the

calories you are burning off and how you can replace them with a chocolate doughnut and double milkshake and you might actually start enjoying yourself.

If you turn out to be a Sports Star, you will be chosen for A Team which leads us on to:

MATCHES
FACT: For a reason which is probably clear only to the Almighty Himself, you will find that the

Under 14s Football Tournament takes place on the coldest day of January and the Junior Cross Country follows the only night this century when four inches of rain fell in 25 minutes.

This will not stop the parents descending in their thousands, standing on the touchline and shouting encouragement or expletives, depending upon the performance of their particular child.

HANDY HINT: One of the Good Things about matches is that you get tea afterwards. Indeed, some of the schools you visit for Away Games will be so keen to impress that they go overboard and pile on the salmon sandwiches, Danish pastries and chocolate wagon wheels with gay abandon. The staff insist that the whole occasion is intended to encourage social intercourse (I said social) between the pupils but who can conduct an intelligent conversation with a mouth jammed full of cinnamon doughnut? Added to that, the parents get invited and you are likely to double up with mirth at the sight of Mr Chamberlain–Whitehead slapping his son on the back and crying "Terrific tackle, Thomas" or Mrs Duncorn mopping away a tear at the sheer joy of little Geraldine's second goal.

Speaking of the parents, a word of warning. In recent years there appears to have been an upsurge in Parent versus Pupil matches. It's all this Comic Relief and Children in Need fundraising that does it. Now if the thought of the maternal parent hurling her 44 inch chest around a rounders pitch fills you with a sense of imminent doom, act quickly. As soon as the event is mentioned, get your mother roped in for something safe, like serving the ice cream or being in charge of Elastoplast. It saves a lot of embarrassment all round.

EXAMS AND HOW TO SURVIVE THEM

"Do not on any account attempt to write on both sides of the paper at once."
W. C. Sellar and R. Yeatman

At the end of the day, no matter how you look at it, you are at school to learn. And to remember. And it is this last bit that causes all the problems. So they have exams. That way, those in charge can find out which of their pupils remembers why $x = y \times 4t$ and which haven't a clue what x is in the first place.

Not everyone approaches exams in the same way and not everyone revises in the same way. It does help if you can identify what sort of examinee you are and how to get the best out of yourself without inducing a nervous breakdown.

THE PETRIFIED

These are the people for whom the word "exam" induces a massive upsurge in heart rate, clammy palms and a desire to run very far away and never come back. Never mind that all through the term they can get 8 out of 10 without even trying; sit them in a silent classroom with a clock ticking away the minutes and a pile of spotless white paper before them, and everything they ever knew vanishes from their minds.

If you are one of these, here is what to do:

1) About three weeks before the exams, sit yourself down firmly and have a chat with yourself. What is an exam? A test. How many tests do you have every term? Dozens. How do you get on? Fine. Right, so why worry because they have called this one an exam? Would you stop eating burgers if they suddenly called them calorie challenged stomach fillers?

2) Draw up a plan of campaign for the first five minutes of the exam. It is a known fact that 80% of all panicking occurs in the first few moments after the invigilator says, "You may turn your papers over." Count slowly to ten and then back to one. Take three deep breaths and tell yourself that, even if you could not answer a single

question, the sun would still rise tomorrow, life would go on and you would have another chance. There is always another chance; you never blow life in one go.

YOU MAY TURN YOUR PAPERS OVER

THE DISORGANISED

This is the soul who works flat out for German literature for days on end and then wakes up to discover that German isn't till next week and she has two hours to master three terms of Physics. This species is also likely to start re-reading Vanity Fair (the book) and then find a fascinating piece about highlights in Vanity Fair (the magazine) and waste a whole evening.

This is what you do:

1) Draw up a timetable. Set yourself one hour for a specific topic and then schedule yourself a 15 minute break. That break can be used for anything from making Marmite and cheese spread sandwiches (marvellous for the brainpower) to defuzzing your legs. But when it is over, it is back for the second hour.

2) Find a study partner. That may sound frightfully Summer Bay, but if you are not the most orderly person, it can be a real bonus to have a friend who is studying the same subjects to keep you on the straight and narrow. Again, allow yourself little treats during the evening, and nag each other into completing the task in hand.

THE COCKY

"Exams? A doddle. I can't think what you are bothering for."

Yes, there are people for whom two hours of Latin translation is as easy as the Sun crossword and aren't they the lucky ones? Don't let them persuade you into dashing off round the shops or watching Bodyguard on video when you should be sorting out your cliff formations and flora of the Mississippi swamplands. They have their uses, however. When you are feeling that you will never get the hang of the hypotenuse, take them for a doughnut and coke: they'll explain it to you and feel all warm and smug inside and you might just comprehend. And if you don't you've had a nice break anyway.

BOOSTING THE BRAIN POWER – STUDY AIDS TO KEEP YOU SANE

1. Peace and quiet. Persuade younger brother to desist from practising Kung Fu kicks against the bedroom wall and ask Father to postpone his renovation of the kitchen cabinets till next month. Having got them to comply, don't have Guns and Roses blaring forth – they might feel a bit miffed. Soft background music suits some

people – others. Do what is right for you.

2. Plenty of nibbles. Suggestions include Marmite and cheese spread sandwiches, celery sticks with lashings of peanut butter, chocolate digestive biscuits, apples, polo mints, bananas.

This is not the time to worry too much about the Health and Fitness regime – if coffee keeps you going or hot chocolate with cinnamon on the top fires your brain cells, so be it. The time for dieting is not now.

3. Work out a timetable for study and stick to it. It's no good sitting down for hours looking at your books if you haven't got a worthwhile scheme of revision.

4. Someone to talk to. When you get that desperate feeling of doom in the pit of your stomach, it helps to talk to someone. Your mum, big sister, next-door neighbour – anyone who has been there, seen it, done it and got the T-shirt. It helps restore a sense of perspective to the whole thing.

PICK UP YOUR PENS...

Don't listen to all the people who swear they studied for 18 hours a day for the past three months. Nor those who say they never opened a book. People always exaggerate.

The worst thing about exams is the atmosphere. Sitting there in regimented rows, in a doom-laden silence broken only by the sound of Kevin McGurk's hiccups and the air bubbles clonking through the ancient radiator, it is very hard to think positive cheerful thoughts. Add to that the invigilator, with an expression set in stone, pacing up and down the aisles to make sure no-one is cheating/disappearing/going to be sick, and you have the makings of a horror movie. Don't let it get to you. Build an invisible bubble around yourself and let the rest of the room get on with it. Oh and by the way, don't have orange juice for breakfast – it plays havoc with bladder control.

THE POST-MORTEM

I could say don't have one, but everyone does, so what would be the point? Don't let it worry you too much if half your friends thought the answer to question 5 was 88 hours and you got 32 minutes. Don't panic if your interpretation of the poems of Wilfred Owen bears no relation to anyone else's: interpretation is a very individual thing. Once the exam is over there is precious little you can do about it so try not to relive every question in your mind for the next five hours. Start panicking about the next exam instead.

THE RESULTS

Unless you are a budding Einstein, there will always be people who have done better than you. And usually, several who have done a lot worse. Only you will know in your heart of hearts whether you could have done better. If you could, don't worry; you will next time. If not, you gave your all and that in itself is something to be proud of.

EXAM RESULTS

KEVIN McGURK :

ART — TOTALLY BRILL

ENGLISH — BRILL

BIOLOGY — ACE

GEOGRAPHY — MEGA

CHEMISTRY — OH DEAR

PHYSICS — O.K.

HISTORY — NOT O.K.
FRENCH — NO WAY!
MATHS — SAD

Chapter Seven
SOJOURNS IN THE SICK ROOM

"Are you sick or are you sullen?"
(Samuel Johnson)

The first time you get to school and suddenly realise that you are about to eject your entire breakfast over the Biology lab floor, will give you your first encounter with the mysteries of The Office and The San. Ill though you may be feeling, it is imperative that you handle this with care.

HOW ILL IS ILL?

When any form of illness strikes, your teacher will dispatch you as fast as possible to the Office. There are things you should know.

1. The School Secretary, who has seen it all before, will not be remotely impressed when you tell her you are dying. Indeed, such may be the

extent of her compassion that she will finish
typing her letter to the Chairman of the PTA
before even raising her eyes to your pallid visage.

2. She will then demand, "Why did you come to
school?" They all say this - it must be written
down in the Guidelines for School Secretaries
Facing Sick Kids. You have a variety of replies.

(i)   *The flippant excuse:* "Because it's Tuesday."
This is probably the truest but there again they
will note you down as insolent and say that if you
have the strength to be so witty you can't be
properly ill.
(ii)   *The real truth:* "My mother made me." After
all, having watched you down two bowls of
Wheatyloops, a fried egg sandwich and a Passion
Fruit and Mango yoghurt, the poor woman could
hardly be blamed for assuming that your inner
workings were in order. However, you do not
want to present your parent as a hard-hearted
despot or yourself as a wimp.
(iii) *The winning excuse.* "I felt fine at breakfast
time." Top marks for truth and it implies that the
source of your incredibly debilitating illness lies
within the portals of the school itself. Tell them
you started to feel ill after having a drink of water
from the drinking fountain and terminal panic

will set in. Add that the weird smell emanating from the Chemistry lab added to your nausea and it will be Red Alert throughout the building.

Faced with your valiant attempts at martyrdom and not quite certain what to believe, the secretary, who is after all paid to type timetables and write to governors and not to diagnose rampant malaria, will send you post-haste to the School Nurse. This means going to the Sick Room.

THE SICK ROOM

Usually painted in shades of sludge, fading magnolia or khaki green – this could be in order to enable the puke to blend in with the surrounding emulsion, or maybe it is supposed to be soothing. The effect is dismal in the extreme – perhaps they think it will encourage you to get better, if only to leave the place.

Your progress from now on depends largely on Nurse or Sister or whatever they call her. There are three main types.

THE IRON LADY
Nothing to do with politics. Usually getting on in

years and liable to look at you with a degree of suspicion more suited to the Inns of Court than a secondary school. Quite why she should imagine that you would pretend to have galloping diarrhoea or a burst eardrum in order to spend a few scintillating hours in her Unwell Room deprived of all social intercourse, one cannot imagine. However, the interrogation that follows suggests that she cannot believe that any form of genuine illness would dare to show its face within her portals.

Nurse: "What hurts?"
Ailing You: "Well nothing actually hurts – I just...."

Nurse: "Then why are you here?"
Rapidly Expiring You: "I was sick."
Softening Nurse: "And do you still feel sick?"

AT THIS POINT THINK HARD: Say "yes" and
it's the grey blanketed bed and a bright yellow
plastic bucket smelling of Jeyes Fluid; say "no"
and be accused of malingering and packed off to
Physics. Your best bet is "A bit" and add a
headache for good measure. They worry a lot
about headaches, what with meningitis and
concussion and all sorts, and invariably ring for
your mother in order to place the ball firmly in
her court if your condition worsens.

THE EARTH MOTHER
A much gentler sort of soul altogether, but don't
make the mistake of assuming she is a soft touch.
She can tell Malingerers from Genuine Diseases
at 50 paces. However, she is also human enough
and has enough sense to know that even kids
who malinger have a reason, and she is perfectly
happy to settle down in an armchair and offer
you a malted milk biscuit and a hot water bottle
and listen to you talk. Within minutes she can
sort out whether your stomach is rebelling after
four lumps of bubble gum have become entwined
in your large intestine or whether the nausea is

97

caused by a Maths teacher who shouts at people who get their hypotenuses in a twist. She likes you to "talk about your problems"; even if you don't have any, make up something mild because she gets terribly upset if she thinks you are withholding anything exciting from her.

THE TRAINEE

From time to time the School Nursing Service hurls an unsuspecting trainee into your midst. Of course, she is accompanied at all times by a fully qualified School Nurse, but in order to get experience she will be left to question you about your ailments using her own initiative. The thing is, she has to be really thorough in case she misses a case of bubonic plague or Black Death, and because she is fired with enthusiasm and a desire to "do well" she will end up asking you the date of your last attack of travel sickness and whether your great aunt suffered from hallucinations. The up side of all this is that she is usually young enough to remember what it was like being at school and is quite happy to sign a sick note so you can have the rest of the day off lessons.

THE SICK NOTE

Speaking of Sick Notes, there are things you should know in order to maximise their very real potential. If you wake up one morning with double vision/peeling skin/measles, your mother will scrawl off a little missive to the school informing them that you won't be attending for a while. No problem. But if you get sent home from school, she still has to send a note if you don't go back the next day. Only she cannot be so creative because the school know what really happened. This is where you come in.

Mother: "I'll tell them it's a mild stomach upset."
Mild? No way. Never admit to anything being mild. It plays the whole thing down too much and rules out any chance of you getting out of netball, furniture moving or anything else once you are back.
You: "How about suspected food poisoning?"
This time the parent refuses. After all it suggests that she doesn't keep her fridge clean or feeds you burgers which have passed their sell-by date.

To cut a long story short, if you have been sick call it mesenteric adenitis. Wonderful, that, because no one at school will know what it is, it sounds fearfully cool and gives you the chance to play on it for at least five days. If anyone does check with the doctor, it really exists – it's another name for – well, being sick, really.

Any other ailment such as headaches, rashes, muscle fatigue and hot flushes can be put down to a "non-specific virus". This basically means that no one knows what the hell is the matter with you, but it will probably go away soon. Of course, you can always then suffer from post-viral fatigue and be off games for another week.

"BUNKOFFITIS". This disease, well known to 11–18 year olds, covers all ailments created in the imagination of the so-called sufferer as a way of getting out of (or bunking off) anything they don't want to do.

Everyone does it occasionally; only idiots try it on too often. After all, just how many verrucae can one left foot sustain? And there is also the real risk of crying wolf. One 14 year old of my acquaintance had claimed vague injuries in netball so often, that when she did dislocate her index finger, it took her ten minutes to convince her games teacher that this was for real.

FOOTNOTE: If you feel ill, and it is genuine, don't try to be brave. Tell someone straight away.

99 times out of 100 it will be the beginnings of
flu/the end of last night's Vindaloo/chickenpox.
But you just might have something that needs
immediate attention.

Chapter Eight
THE PARENTS' EVENING
(or Close Encounters of the Worst Kind)

"Why are we never quite at ease in the presence of a
schoolmaster?"
(Charles Lamb)

After you have been at school a couple of terms, a
new joy will be thrust upon you and your family,
the Parents' Evening. In some schools, the
parents will be invited to chat with the staff while
you sit at home watching telly and worrying about
what they are saying behind your back. In more
progressive "Let's all be one big happy family"
schools, you will be asked to go along as well. It is
debatable whether it is better to be there, where
you can keep an eye on what is going on and put
your oar in when necessary, or to be at home
where you don't have to hear what they are saying
about you.

WHEN YOU ARE INCLUDED

Taking parents anywhere is a risk: letting them

loose in a room full of teachers is fraught with danger. For one thing, they are all on the same side – the "getting the best out of the boy/girl" team. You need to know what you are letting yourself in for.

TAKING YOUR TURN

You will get a note informing your parents that they have five minutes with each member of staff in order to facilitate the maximum flow of bodies. It sounds like a very good idea but it never works. There you are, with the freshly combed Father, queuing patiently to see the Head of French while the parents of Cecilia Descartes are holding forth at great length about their child's Mediterranean background, her penchant for languages and her sensitive nature. Poor Mr K makes weak and ineffectual attempts to draw the conversation to a close. You and your parents have three courses of action:

1.   Move to another queue. No good; the same thing will repeat itself, only this time it will be Mr Vocal thumping his fist on the table and demanding to know why Jeremy is not in the top set for English.

2.   Pretend that you are about to faint, in the

hope that Mother Descartes will remove her buttocks from the chair and let you collapse into it and make a rapid recovery.

3. Go home. (Not good, this – it labels your family as uninterested and that is a very rude word in the staffroom.)

Whatever you do, try to prevent the by now weary parent from complaining out loud. Remarks such as "If I ran my business like they run a Parents' Evening, we would all be bankrupt" are unlikely to endear your family to the Head.

Once you get to see the teacher in question, there are more hazards to be overcome.

1. Getting found out. Remember all those little white lies you told your father? Like the C that you pushed up to a B minus? Or the Maths test that you said you got 7 out of 10 for because 4 didn't sound very good? Well, I can promise you that Mrs Higgins will take great delight in producing said piece of work from her little black folder and offering it to the parents to read. You will notice a tightening of the paternal lip and a heightening of the maternal cheek colour. This means trouble when you get home. The only remedy is to come clean in future. It saves an awful lot of hassle later.

2. Handling the conversation. Different teachers have different approaches to Parents' Evening. Some will gush and grovel to your parents in such a sickening manner that you have a keen desire to throw up; others will try to impress with their aloof superiority; and yet others will seem totally bored.

WHEN YOU ARE LEFT AT HOME

While at first sight, sitting at home watching The

New Baywatch seems infinitely preferable to
sitting at school hearing about your failed
Geography exam, it is not without its problems.

1. By the time your parents get home, they are
tired, have sore bottoms from sitting on school
chairs with sagging seats and are gasping for a
coffee. If they have heard good reports of you,
they will pat you on the back, tell you to keep it
up and let you go to bed. If they are worried
about your algebra, batting averages and grasp of
European History, they will want to talk. Be
patient with them.

2. Parents do worry. It is a fact of life, like
autumn following summer and tights only
laddering where it shows. If they nag a bit about
your work, don't stamp your feet/scream/throw
the TV Times at them. If it's bad because you
don't understand, say so. If it's bad because the
subject holds no interest, tell them. And if you
know it's just because you've been a bit lazy,
confess. They'll be far more understanding than
you imagine.

3. Say "Thanks for going." No, I am not going
loopy – some parents just don't bother to go,
which makes their kids feel a bit left out. You

might not like the speech on neat handwriting and learning to spell that follows, but at least they show they care.

While I doubt there are more than a handful of kids and parents who can put their hands on their hearts and swear that they love Parents' Evenings (except the mummy and daddy of William the Whizz Kid who gets straight A's and never misses the goal-post), they are there to be endured. And remember, your parents will be dreading them as much as you. After all, whose genes is it that determine your brain power?

THEY DO HAVE A POINT

Before you bite your parents' heads off or write your teacher off as a nag, remember, they do have a point. They've been there, done it and got the T-shirt. And what's more, believe it or not, they know what you can do and are there to make sure you do it.

MR McGURK + MRS McGURK

= KEVIN

Chapter Nine
CONVERSATIONAL GAMBITS
'or Learning Teacher-Speak'

"When I say a word," Humpty said in a rather
scornful tone, *"It means just what I choose it to mean
– neither more nor less."*
Lewis Carroll

Considering that they spend a large part of every
day telling you to write clearly, speak up and say
what you have to say, you would expect them to
say what they mean and mean what they say. But
they don't. Not on Parents' Evenings or when
writing school reports anyway. Here is a little help
in sussing out just what they are getting at:

What they say: "Elaine expresses herself easily and
fluently."
What they probably mean: Elaine talks a lot and
never shuts up.

What they say: "While realising that Amanda is
not a keen sportswoman, she must learn to show
a little more thrust on the hockey pitch."

What they probably mean: Amanda is now too old too burst into tears every time the ball touches her big toe.

What they say: "We are puzzled by Gavin's obvious difficulty in understanding Ordinance Survey symbols."
What they probably mean: How in the name of heaven does he find his way home at night?

What they say: "It would be advisable for Alex to concentrate on the consolidation of basic mathematical principles before the end of year examinations."
What they probably mean: Alex would be advised to learn to count.

What they say: "While pleased that Miranda is showing more interest in History, she must learn to concentrate her efforts on the more relevant parts of the syllabus."
What they probably mean: The finer details of the sex life of Henry VIII, while fascinating, is not required at GCSE.

What they say: "Lisa is fully occupied in the extra-curricular life of the school."
What they probably mean: Perhaps she could force herself to find some time for study as well.

The art of tactful self-expression is one that you too will need as the first year progresses. There follows a few tips on getting your message across – subtly.

NOW LET ME PUT IT THIS WAY...
(or ways of telling parents unpalatable truths)

What you say: "I didn't come bottom in Maths."
What you mean: I came next to bottom in Maths.

What you say: "It wasn't my fault, honestly."
What you mean: All the evidence points to the fact that it was my fault.

What you say: "Mrs Matthews said my Geometry is improving."
What you mean: Kate Higgins got my prep right this week.

What you say: "I'm starving."
What you mean: I gave my packed lunch to Kate in exchange for the Geometry homework.

What you say: "Would it be possible for Charlie to spend the night?"
What you mean: Charlie is in the hallway with her suitcase.

What you say: "I've finished my homework."
What you mean: I've finished the two questions I can do and it's time for Top of the Pops.

What you say: "I'm really getting to like Chemistry."
What you mean: So don't be too mad when the bill arrives for the repairs to the hole in the floorboards.

What you say: "Would you like a cup of tea?"
What you mean: Could I have a sleepover party for 15 tomorrow?

What you say: "If you let me have the party, we won't make any mess and I won't ever ask for anything again."
What you mean: Maybe.

Chapter Ten
SCHOOL TRIPS
(or Don't be sick on the driver)

"Travel is a part of education"
(Bacon)

The Trips are one of the highlights of the academic year. These range from a morning out at a sewage farm (definitely a one-star excursion), through a weekend hunting fossils on Chesil Beach (two stars) to a week in Germany (three stars).

THE DAY TRIP
A day away from the routine of lessons and school bells is very appealing. Somehow it is much easier to understand electricity when you have been round a power station, or to develop an interest in Roman History when you have stood in the ruins of a Roman bathroom.

COACH CRED
The back seat is best and is filled first. It's not

brilliant if you are a bad traveller, but is great for looking out the back window at the talent following behind in the red Ferrari and keeps you out of immediate eye contact with those in charge.

Avoid seats over the wheels if you are likely to feel queasy. If you do feel sick, don't just sit there. Ask the driver to stop. Do not do this if opening your mouth means jettisoning your breakfast all over the poor man. Do it in a carrier bag instead.

Don't sit too near the front unless you want the teacher in charge holding forth for 50 miles about the breadth of Shakespearian language/the workings of a power station/the joys of Monet. If you do get lumbered with this seat, look enormously interested for ten minutes and then say "I must make some notes" and write to your letter to your penfriend in Ormesson–sur–Marne. Or you could always feign sleep.

Remember the number of your coach; hunting for your mates in the car park at Wembley at 8pm on a rainy November evening is no fun.

CLIPBOARD CRED
FACT: You get given a clipboard and a pencil and are sent hurtling round town to assess shopping trends/round a farm to assess agricultural trends/round a museum answering

questions about dead people.

FACT: There is always one rogue clipboard in every allocation. You will probably get it. You spend the morning either desperately trying to clamp your paper down, or running marathons round town chasing sheets of information which are blowing in the wind.

FACT: Clipboards can be a dead giveaway. If your teacher finds tomato ketchup stains on your answer about the number of car parking spaces in Romford, she might just guess that you spent half the morning in MacDonalds.

Take spare pencils (in case of breakage) and a polythene bag in case it rains. No, not for your head – for the clipboard.

THE THEATRE TRIP

Usually to see a play that you are studying for GCSE or A level. Don't knock it: King Lear never makes sense till you see it at Stratford. Some schools broaden your horizons with trips to the ballet, orchestral concerts or alternative theatre. Give it all a go before you say "Yuck".

*DON'T talk and rustle sweet papers during the performance or giggle at the bit where Juliet dies.
*DO keep the programme – the footnotes come

in very handy when you have to right an essay about the effectiveness of the staging in A Man for all Seasons.

THE WEEKEND FIELD TRIP

Definitely for the stout of mind and body, this. If it's a biology trip it will all be about ecology and the preservation of terrestrial life and if it's Geography it's glaciation in Snowdonia or fossils at Chesil Beach. Either way, there is a risk of gashed kneecaps, blisters, wet hair, mud under the fingernails and incipient bronchial pneumonia.

Many of these field trips are based either in little wooden huts in country field centres or under canvas, quite often near to a herd of grazing cattle.

CAMPING CRED

DO take double the number of socks you think you will need. Rain, cowpats and pools on the seashore can wreak havoc with the footwear.

DO take antiseptic cream and plasters – you get blisters climbing Pen-y-Fan in walking boots that haven't been on for two years.

DO take Victory V's to suck in force 10 gales and plenty of high-energy snacks. It can be a long time between breakfast and lunch when you are measuring soil erosion.

DON'T forget to take some coins and a phonecard – that way you can phone home if you have a pang of homesickness, want to talk to the cat or just feel like a natter.

119

THE OVERSEAS TRIP

With the barriers tumbling down all over Europe, the school exchange has an even more vital role to play than before. The idea is that you and your pals hurtle over to France or Germany or Italy or some such and the foreign kids come here and savour the joys of an English education. Prior to your departure for foreign fields, there are some things you should know.

EUROCRED

1. DON'T expect a lie-in in the mornings. Continental kids go to school very early. You will be out of bed by 6.30am with your first lesson at 8am. The up side of this is that they finish at 2pm.

2. DON'T look for a cooked breakfast. If you are a bacon, egg, sausage and tomato person in the mornings, tough luck. The French gobble a croissant with jam and drink what resembles a small washbasin full of milky coffee; the Germans grab some strange-looking *brot* with a dollop of *wurst* and eat it on the run. Smuggle Marmite into your schoolbag.

120

3. DON'T worry about the school. If you have been used to a fairly strict regime at your own school, you are in for a surprise. In Germany in particular there is precious little discipline and the classroom atmosphere is casual. Your teacher will be at pains to point out that this is not an excuse for you to be rude or rowdy. Self-discipline, rather than the imposed variety, is the order of the day. Many teachers return to the UK smugly pleased with the very kids they were reprimanding for noisiness the month before.

121

4. DO go on all the visits. You will get taken around to all manner of educationally stimulating sites and probably introduced to the mayor of the town in which you are staying. This is quite jolly: you give him a book about your home town and he gives you one about his and then you all have a glass of Liebfraumilch and a slice of strudel, slap one another on the backs and cry "Auf wiedersehen" and go shopping.

Visits often include factories (good for free samples), the police station (great for Rogues' Gallery), art galleries and radio stations.

Then you get free time to do your own thing. Like sampling local beer, eating red cabbage and doing the funfairs.

5. DO pack the essentials: a small but typically English present for your host family; a phrase book (even your German probably won't stretch to the answer to "What do you think of the newly-structured Bundesbank?"); postcards of your home town to give away; Marmite.

THE SKI TRIP
Brilliant fun even if you can't do it and spend most of the time on your back in the snow. If you do happen to tumble base over apex and break or dislocate something, you often get given

Gluhwein to ease the pain while they carry you down the mountain. My daughter got that treatment and giggled hysterically all the way to the hospital.

Ski trips are not cheap – if your parents can't afford to let you go this year, work like crazy and save up for another year. You can hire all the kit, right down to the goggles and gloves – good idea for a Christmas present?

THE CRUISE
Some schools go on Mediterranean cruises which are very expensive but wonderful. Save for months cleaning cars, polishing your grandmother, and cat–sitting for Aunt Flo, but get there if you can. The staff will tell you all about the glories of Athens and the treasures of Tutankhamun, which are amazing and unforgettable, but don't miss the apple tea in Turkey, camel rides and papyrus factories in Egypt and Dead Sea Mud (brilliant for dispensing with acne.)

AND APRES...
Needless to say, you won't get off lightly after all this travel and jollity. You will write countless essays about what you did, where you did it, what you thought about it after you had done it and

whether you would do it again. You will be detailed to supply photographs for the school magazine, collages for the Day Room and information packs for next year's students. But it's worth it.

Chapter Eleven
A–Z OF BOARDING

A is for *Assisted Place*. Some schools are part of this government scheme which helps the parents of bright children pay for the tuition element of the school fees. It can be a great help if your dad is made redundant halfway through your school career.

B is for *Boarding House*. There will be several boarding houses, and in addition to dormitories, they have a day room. Check this out for television, comfortable chairs, kettle, toaster and hopefully a microwave. In things like Drama, Music and Sports they often have inter-house competitions. Good for getting in a team without having to take on the whole school at trials.

C is for *Combined Cadet Force*. This one-time male preserve now takes girls. You can join the Army, Navy or Air Force sections and leap around one afternoon a week resembling contestants for the Krypton Factor as you risk life and limb in the cause of *mens sana in corpore sano*. (Although where sanity comes in when you are turning upside down in a canoe in mid February, heaven knows.) There are courses on everything from modern weaponry to survival, but the best course is orienteering because you can pretend to get lost and pop into Burger King for a Whopper on the way.

D is for *Dormitories*. Since you will be sleeping here for ten weeks at a stretch, they need to be homely and well equipped. Good signs include plenty of mirrors, private cupboard space, personal duvet covers, lots of soft toys, posters covering the walls, private lockers, and carpet or rugs. Bad signs to watch for include old-fashioned iron beds, bare boards, a chill in the air, and lists pinned to the walls saying "Pupils shall not ..."

E is for *Exeats*. Twice a term you get an Exeat (that's Latin for he, she or it goes out). If you live near enough, you can go home, re-acquaint yourself with your parents, the cat and the contents of your mother's freezer, have a long hot bath without anyone shouting "Time" and persuade your father to up your allowance to accommodate a pair of Gap reverse fit jeans without which your street cred will be as nothing.

If your parents are in Dubai or Darwin, one of your friends will in all probability invite you to their place. Take a bunch of flowers for their mum; this labels you "a very nice person" and means you get invited again and no-one minds

when you eat four slices of Passion Cake.

F is for *Food*. Although it is heaps better than it used to be, boarding school food never quite comes up to the standards of home. Some do brilliant breakfasts and fall down on puddings;

others are great on after-match teas but hopeless on the meat and two veg. However, all schools have subsidised Tuck Shops and you won't die of malnutrition in ten weeks.

G is for *Grounds*. Most boarding schools have large grounds. This is particularly important because everyone needs some time to just wander and think. The tennis courts and other facilities will be available for use in the evening. No big deal if you have your own swimming pool at home, but it beats queuing at the Sports Centre any day.

H is for *Homesickness*. You will get it at first. Nearly everyone does. For some it lasts a week or so and only resurfaces on birthdays, when you feel ill or when you miss the budgie. For others, it takes longer to overcome and you feel as if life is not worth living. But you will get over it. Talk about it to your friends, teachers, and housemistress or master. You are not unique: it's the people who don't get homesick who are different.

I is for *Illness*. Being ill away from home is no fun, and everyone knows that. Most boarding schools have a Sanatorium where you sleep while you are infectious in the hope that the bugs won't spread. If you are likely to be ill for long, you will usually be allowed to go home.

J is for *Jollifications* and *Junketings*. Boarding schools love these. Parents, governors and friends get invited to everything from Barn Dances to Barbecues. After speech day, your parents usually get Cheese and Wine (or whine if you did not get a prize). Trouble is, it's the kids who get roped in to stick bits of cheese on top of bits of pineapple, to serve the punch and be generally charming to all and sundry.

K is for *Kit Sales*. A great way of keeping costs down. You sell off your outgrown uniform or unwanted textbooks at bargain prices. You get some cash, the purchaser gets a bargain and everyone is happy.

L is for *Lights Out*. Usually based on age and ranging from 9.30 to 11pm. You may think this is pretty unfair if you don't happen to be tired, but the person in the next bed may be shattered. You could try a torch under the bedclothes or a trip to the loo with Just 17 tucked into your pyjamas. But after two hours of hockey, an essay on photosynthesis, Wind Band practice and a mile hike to town to buy your mum's birthday card, you may wish lights out was at 8pm.

M is for *Money*. Sending you to boarding school will cost an arm and a leg. In addition to the fees, there is the uniform, the phone calls home, the theatre trips and so on. Make the most of your time there and don't be surprised if your parents don't decorate the sitting room for five years. In case of hardship, see Assisted Places above.

N is for *Noise*. It takes time to get used to being with a crowd of people all day and all night. At first you will wake up every time someone coughs.

Within two weeks you will sleep through three morning bells and a passing fire engine.

O is for *Outings*. You get a lot of outings at boarding school. Staff arrange bowling evenings, skating evenings and trips to the cinema. In fact, you may get out more than you do at home.

P is for *Prefects*. They have charge of things like lights out, making rotas for keeping the day room tidy, organising house matches and so on. It is also for *Privileges* which come with being a Prefect such as staying up later, wearing your own clothes or being allowed to use the kitchen.

Q is for *Quiet Moments*. This is something you may miss if you have not been used to sharing a bedroom with three others, eating breakfast with 400 and waiting for your turn on the rota to have a bath. When it gets to you, find a corner of the playing field and give yourself half an hour alone.

R is for *Rules*. Check these carefully. Make sure that you are allowed to phone home when you need to (within reason); receive incoming calls at pre-arranged times; take personal possessions like stereos, family photographs and pictures, and go into town at least twice a week.

S is for *Speech Day*. Handle with care. Seat your parents near the mother and father of someone rather dim. There is nothing worse for your mother than being placed next to someone whose child has carried off the Mathematics Prize, Bowler of the Year cup, Encyclopedia for Service to the School and the Ponsonby-Young Memorial Prize. Particularly if all you got was Runner-Up in the Long Jump. The presentation of prizes is usually followed by a Jollification and Junketing. (See J above.)

T is for *Tuck Box*. At the start of every term you are allowed to take a Tuck Box to school stocked with your mother's chocolate fudge cake, dozens of packets of crisps and a mountain of sweets. After two days when all that has gone, you rely on the Tuck Shop. Usually stocks everything from cheese rolls to hot drinks. Great during exam revision time when the only thing that keeps you going is a regular infusion of honey-coated peanuts. Try offering to help out occasionally – that way you have access to supplies and can snap up leftovers at knockdown prices.

U is for *Uniform*. Some top-class boarding schools still have things like capes or velvet knickerbockers but thankfully these are in the minority and are only for special occasions. In addition to blazers and panama hats and overcoats, you will need an assortment of casual clothes. Jeans are allowed but some prospectuses carry little footnotes along the lines of "T shirts bearing slogans, and jeans with frayed legs will not be allowed." Do take lots of thick sweaters; bursars tend to creep around turning radiators down to save funds and most public schools were built in the days when it was believed that freezing to death was character-building.

V is for *Visits*. Most schools are perfectly happy to allow visits from family and friends at set times. The days when kids were banished to boarding school and never saw their families for weeks are long gone. Visitors usually take you out to eat, which is good, and leave cash behind, which is better.

W is for *Weekly Boarding*. The best of both worlds. You stay at school from Sunday evening till Friday teatime and spend the weekend at home. Great if you live nearby but you do tend to miss out on the social life of the school.

X is for – well, you think of something.

Y is for *You*. You are a very important person – *the* important person in your life. If at any time you think boarding school is not working out for you, or you have problems you simply can't handle, tell your parents. They won't force you to stay if things are that bad.

Z is for *Zombie* which is what most first time boarders feel like for a week or two. What with lying awake at night because you are missing your golden labrador, struggles with the rules of lacrosse and getting gnawing pains in your stomach because you couldn't face the solidified macaroni cheese, you may think life is going to be hell. Then one day you wake up find two weekend invitations in your locker and discover you've been picked to play Juliet opposite the sexiest chap in school. From then on life's a breeze.

So there you have it. All you have to do now is grit your teeth, sharpen your pencils and your wit and go for it. You can knock 'em dead if you try – and enjoy yourself in the process.

Remember – have fun, work hard, play hard, and soak up as many new experiences as you can. And never forget what old Mark Twain said: "I have never let my schooling interfere with my education."